CW01512594

Original title:
Obsidian Sheets Inside the Mermaid Vent

Author: Kätriin Kaldaru
ISBN HARDBACK: 978-1-80563-127-9
ISBN PAPERBACK: 978-1-80564-648-8

Silken Shadows of the Sunken Path

Beneath the boughs of ancient trees,
A whisper dances on the breeze,
With secrets held in twilight's gleam,
The sunken path weaves through a dream.

Mist drapes softly, cloaking the way,
Where shadows linger, muted and gray,
In tangled roots, the stories hide,
Of wanderers lost to time's great tide.

Echoes flicker like fireflies bright,
Illuminating the depths of night,
With each step taken, you might find,
The echoes call from the back of your mind.

Gnarly branches twist and entwine,
Guarding secrets of fate's design,
As silken shadows brush your skin,
And another world pulls you in.

In whispered tones, the path will share,
Of hopes and fears, of love laid bare,
So tread with care on this hallowed ground,
For in its hold, truth can be found.

Underwater Dreams in the Depths of Night

Beneath the moon's soft silver glow,
Where shadows dance with ebb and flow,
The ocean whispers secrets low,
In dreams of depths we long to know.

With creatures gliding, fierce and bright,
They weave through currents, heart's delight,
In silence, stars blink out their light,
As dreams unfold, taking flight.

Coral towers reach for the sky,
In a realm where thoughts dare to fly,
Their colors burst, they shimmer by,
Where fantasies with waters tie.

So dive into the midnight blue,
Where every tale feels strangely true,
In dreams, the ocean sings to you,
Embracing all that you pursue.

With every wave, a story's spun,
From battles fought to love begun,
A journey deep where fears are none,
In underwater realms, we run.

Reflections in a Murky Glasslike Sea

A surface calm, a mirrored face,
Where thoughts can drift without a trace,
In murky depths, they find their place,
In secrets held, they'll leave a space.

As shadows flicker, shapes appear,
From whispered tales that fill with fear,
The glassy tide, both dark and clear,
It holds the past that lingers near.

An echo calls from deep below,
Where mysteries in silence flow,
Reflections dance in ebb and glow,
In depths of night, they surely grow.

With every ripple, memories blend,
In currents strong, both foe and friend,
A journey long that may not end,
In waters deep, our hearts we send.

So gaze upon the sea's embrace,
Find in its depths a soothing grace,
In murky tides, we choose to trace,
The stories etched in time and space.

Enigmas within the Nautical Abyss

In darkest night, where silence reigns,
The abyss holds its ancient claims,
With every sound, a puzzle gains,
In depths where time forgets its chains.

Here creatures murmur, lost in lore,
Of sunken ships and treasures sore,
With echoes of the ocean's roar,
They rise and fall on unseen shore.

Whispers call from caverns deep,
For secrets cradled, shadows keep,
In barnacle homes where dwellers seep,
The enigmatic tides, they sweep.

In chambers dark, where few have trod,
The unexplored, where dreams are flawed,
Each wave, a story, rich and broad,
In mysteries that we applaud.

So dare to delve where fears take flight,
In the heart of the endless night,
For enigmas wait, not out of sight,
Within the abyss, our souls ignite.

Midnight's Caress on Waters Unseen

As shadows wrap the day in night,
The ocean breathes with soft delight,
A lullaby, a whispered flight,
In midnight's arms, the stars are bright.

The tides embrace the moon's sweet glow,
Each wave, a brush that dances slow,
With strokes of dreams, we come to know,
The gentle touch of night's soft flow.

In hidden coves, where silence sways,
The world beneath, in quiet plays,
With rhythms drawn from silent bays,
As midnight weaves through shadowed ways.

With every ripple, hearts unseal,
In waters calm, we start to feel,
The magic of the night revealed,
Where dreams and ocean's force congeal.

So let the night wrap you in peace,
In midnight's caress, find release,
As waters whisper, fears all cease,
In unseen realms, our spirits cease.

Shattered Gleams of Ocean Dreams

In twilight's glow the waves do break,
A dance of light, a soft heartache.
Beneath the foam, lost dreams do lie,
Embraced by whispers of the sky.

With every crest, a tale unfolds,
Of sailors brave and treasures bold.
Reflections spark, then fade away,
As night enfolds the dying day.

Soft silver fish in harmony swim,
Their fleeting paths both bright and dim.
The ocean's heart holds secrets deep,
While shadows play, the darkness weep.

Bright shards of hope in deep blue waves,
Glimpse of the past, the future saves.
For in the dark, the tides reveal,
A world of dreams that gently heal.

As stars above begin to glow,
The ocean breathes, a tender flow.
In shattered gleams, our wishes rise,
A tapestry of sea and skies.

Deep-Sea Whispers at Twilight

Beneath the waves, a soft refrain,
In twilight's hush, the sea's sweet pain.
Secrets murmur, stories told,
Of ancient realms, of treasures old.

In shadows deep, where silence dwells,
The ocean sings of hidden spells.
Whispers curl like misty threads,
Carrying dreams where magic spreads.

From coral beds, soft voices rise,
A serenade to the starlit skies.
Each drop a note, each wave a song,
In harmony where we belong.

A dance of currents, soft and sly,
Beneath the moon's watchful eye.
The waters weave a mystic art,
Binding souls, not worlds apart.

In this embrace, fears drift away,
As twilight fades, and night holds sway.
Deep-sea whispers weave through air,
A promise lingers, faint and rare.

Celestial Scales of Forgotten Lore

In abyssal depths, the whispers sing,
Of legends lost, and timeless spring.
Celestial scales shine soft and bright,
Guarding lore in endless night.

Every glimmer, a story told,
Of fierce battles and hearts so bold.
In fish and fin, the echoes dwell,
A magic dark, a hidden spell.

From ship to shore, the currents trace,
Footprints left in time and space.
Orbs of light in shadows glance,
Inviting souls to join the dance.

In moonlit tides, the visions blend,
As ages change, yet still transcend.
We seek what lies within the dark,
Amidst the waves, a timeless spark.

With open hearts, we dive below,
To find the tales that ebb and flow.
Celestial scales of lore we claim,
In ocean's depths, we feel the same.

Shadows of the Coral Labyrinth

In coral mazes, shadows play,
Where light and dark weave night with day.
A labyrinth of hues and forms,
Harboring secrets, currents warm.

Each twist and turn, a mystery calls,
Of hidden realms behind the walls.
In pops of color, whispers blend,
Echoes of tales that never end.

With every stroke, the sea unfolds,
Life's vibrant tapestry retold.
In silence deep, the heart does yearn,
For wisdom found at each new turn.

While shadows dance in twilight's breath,
Life coexists with whispers of death.
In this embrace, the wild hearts seek,
A voice of truth, both strong and meek.

So wander down these paths divine,
Where coral whispers intertwine.
Among the shadows brightly seen,
The labyrinth unveils its dream.

Waking the Lament of the Ocean's Soul.

In the hush of dawn's first light,
Whispers drift from depths below,
Tales of sorrow take their flight,
Where only brave souls dare to go.

Ghostly echoes softly rise,
From the heart of azure seas,
Cries of mermaids, lost goodbyes,
Singing low in ancient breeze.

Shadows dance on waves that gleam,
Casting secrets, deep and vast,
In the sky a single beam,
Guiding thoughts of voyages past.

The ocean sighs a heavy sigh,
As the currents weave their art,
A symphony of the sky,
In every shell, a lover's heart.

Yet beneath, the dark secrets sway,
A thousand tales wait to be heard,
As the sun begins to play,
With the depths, in silence stirred.

Abyssal Echoes of Shimmering Depths

Where sunlight fades to muted hue,
The abyss calls with beckoning hands,
A world where only myths are true,
And every ripple silently stands.

In the twilight of the sea's embrace,
Whispers haunt the lonesome caves,
Fading dreams in darkened space,
Guarded by the restless waves.

Shimmering treasures lost to time,
Stories cloaked in sapphire mist,
Voices weaving in pure rhyme,
Of lovers once eternally kissed.

Currents shift with hidden grace,
As the echoes call their tune,
Far beneath the surface's face,
Where shadows dance by the light of the moon.

Each heartbeat thunders in the deep,
Hushed beneath a veil of blue,
Secrets that the ocean keeps,
Await the brave, the bold, the true.

Secrets Beneath the Waves

Beneath the surf and frothy spray,
Lies a realm of whispered dreams,
Hidden gems in shades of grey,
Where the light of history gleams.

Echoing through the watery hall,
Voices call from ages past,
As the currents rise and fall,
The ocean's spell is unsurpassed.

Coral towers tell their tale,
Of battles lost, of love's sweet pain,
Ghostly ships that softly sail,
With longing hearts, like silent grain.

Each shell a story, every grain,
Holds the laughter of the tides,
In the depths, a gentle strain,
Of promises the sea abides.

So dive down through the azure hue,
And listen close as shadows weave,
For the ocean sings a song so true,
A lullaby for those who believe.

Reflections in the Midnight Tide

At midnight's veil, the waters gleam,
Mirrors clash where stars collide,
Each wave a whisper, each wave a dream,
In the depths where secrets slide.

Moonlit paths lead sailors astray,
Their hearts adrift, wild and free,
Caught in the dance of night and day,
Where hopes and fears like shadows flee.

Rippling faces in the night,
Echoes of what came before,
A silent song, a soft twilight,
That calls to wanderers ashore.

Underneath the silver glow,
Mysteries pulse with timeless grace,
And through the tide's relentless flow,
Lovers trace each other's face.

Yet as dawn breaks, the stories fade,
New tales churn beneath the foam,
As the ocean's heart has played,
Its timeless song, forever home.

Sublime Echoes of the Sea's Heart

Whispers of waves greet the shore,
Tales of old in the ocean's roar.
Secrets hidden beneath the tide,
In depths where the dreams and wonders hide.

Pearls of wisdom in shimmering light,
Stars of the sea, twinkling so bright.
Currents dance with a lullaby's tune,
Embracing night like a silvered moon.

A salty breeze carries a song,
Echoes of spirits, where they belong.
Mysteries flow with the ceaseless sea,
As souls entwine, forever free.

In ripples and rippling tales entwine,
Every crest, every trough, a sign.
The heart of the ocean beats so true,
A rhythmic pulse in timeless blue.

When dawn awakens with tender grace,
The horizon blushes, a soft embrace.
And in the silence, the sea's deep thrum,
Calls to our hearts, where we all come from.

Eternal Mysteries of the Ocean's Night

Beneath the cloak of the velvet sky,
The ocean whispers, secrets shy.
Stars reside in its vast embrace,
Nurturing tales of an ancient race.

Moonlight glimmers on swirling waves,
Guarding the paths of hidden caves.
Below the surface, shadows play,
Eternal mysteries dance and sway.

The siren calls with a haunting grace,
Luring sailors to a twilight space.
Notes of longing, so soft, so clear,
Echo through waters, drawing near.

In the depths, where treasures lie,
Whispers of dreams and lullabies.
Fathoms deep, the void does gleam,
A realm of wonder, a sailor's dream.

As tides embrace the night's deep hue,
Infinite wonders call to you.
In the ocean's breath, a promise kept,
In shadows where countless secrets slept.

Siren's Haunt and Shadowed Grace

In twilight's grasp, a voice does sing,
Enchanting hearts, the siren's ring.
With every note, the world stands still,
A binding spell, a timeless thrill.

Her silhouette in moonlit seas,
Haunts the shores with whispered pleas.
A lullaby laced with mystery,
Inviting souls to her history.

Tides shift and swell with her weary heart,
In shadowed grace, a work of art.
Lost to the depths, the dreams take flight,
As shadows weave through the velvet night.

In every wave, a bittersweet tale,
Of longing hearts, of love set sail.
A dance with ghosts on the ocean's crest,
Where time suspends, and hearts find rest.

So listen close when the night winds wail,
To the siren's song, the ocean's trail.
For in her haunt, you've a place to roam,
As every soul seeks its lost home.

Reflections of the Aquatic Veil

In the water's mirror, the world is cast,
A veil of dreams where echoes last.
Ripples ripple through time and space,
Reflections of life in a fluid embrace.

Gentle lapping, a soft refrain,
In currents filled with joy and pain.
The ocean's whispers, a sacred flow,
Every ebb and tide a story to know.

Luminous deep, where shadows glint,
Glories unfold in the subtle hint.
What lies beneath the surface bright?
A tapestry woven with sheer delight.

From the shores, we yearn to behold,
The treasures and secrets the waters hold.
In every splash, a journey unfolds,
In the aquatic veil, the universe molds.

So dive with wonder, let spirits soar,
In depths where the ocean's heart will pour.
With every reflection, a chance to see,
The endless beauty that sets us free.

Celestial Shadows in Undulating Waters

In twilight's shroud where whispers blend,
Shadows dance as stars descend.
The water shimmers, secrets trace,
Reflections hide in silken grace.

Ripples form like dreams unmade,
Telling tales of light and shade.
Celestial orbs in gentle sway,
Guide the night, then fade away.

A lullaby for the lonely heart,
In the dark where visions start.
Each droplet holds a fleeting spark,
A world reborn, a path through dark.

The silent call of the deep unknown,
Awakens echoes, long outgrown.
In currents swift, the shadows twine,
A tapestry of stars divine.

So sail away on dreams of night,
Where shadows weave both dark and light.
In undulating waters wide,
Celestial secrets will abide.

The Moon's Kiss on Still Waters

Upon the lake, the moonlight sighs,
A silver touch that never dies.
Still waters hold a gentle gleam,
Beneath the stars, a whispered dream.

Ripples quiver with every thought,
Messages from the night once sought.
With every breath, the silence speaks,
As time slows down, the soul it seeks.

Reflecting hope in calm embrace,
The moon bestows a soft, sweet grace.
In perfect peace, the heart shall find,
The secrets of the night, entwined.

A serenade for restless hearts,
Where sorrow fades and joy imparts.
The water's hymn, a soothing balm,
A whispered truth, a gentle calm.

So linger by the water's edge,
Where moonbeams dance, and shadows pledge.
In stillness deep, the world is right,
Awash in dreams of silver light.

Silhouettes of Forgotten Tales

In dusty corners of the mind,
Silhouettes of stories bind.
Faded echoes, voices lost,
Each shadow holds a hidden cost.

Once vibrant dreams now draped in gray,
Trace the paths of yesterday.
Forgotten hymns in whispers groan,
In every sigh, a memory's tone.

Figures dance in twilight's shade,
Ghostly forms that time has made.
With every flutter, with every sigh,
The past remembers, oh, so spry.

Bound by threads of joy and pain,
Woven tales like softest rain.
A tapestry of life endured,
In shadows cast, the heart is stirred.

So let us wander through the mist,
And in each outline, find what's missed.
For in the dark, the light still dwells,
The soul awakens—forgotten tales.

Lament of the Sunken Heart

Beneath the waves where sorrows dwell,
The sunken heart begins to swell.
In depths of blue, a mournful sound,
As whispered dreams are lost, unbound.

The ocean's breath, a haunting tune,
Cries out beneath the silver moon.
Each wave that breaks, a tale of woe,
In salty tears, the shadows flow.

A vestige of what once was bright,
Now drowned in endless, starless night.
Drifting hopes like ships at sea,
A ghostly dance of what could be.

Within the depths, the heartbeats fade,
As echoes linger, soft and frayed.
A shadowed pulse that yearns for air,
A silent prayer, a secret care.

Yet in the dark, there flickers light,
A glimmer faint, a spark of fight.
For even in the ocean's grasp,
The sunken heart still dares to clasp.

Veil of the Drowned's Whisper

Beneath the waves where shadows creep,
The secrets of the deep do sleep.
In twilight's grasp, the lost do sigh,
Their whispers blend with ocean's cry.

A shroud of mist, a haunting tune,
The lullabies of sunken moons.
In coral halls where spirits play,
The memories of night and day.

With every swell, a tale unfolds,
In watery graves, the brave and bold.
They dance in rhythm with the tide,
In dreams they weep, in dreams they bide.

Yet hear their call, oh sailor fair,
For not all dreams are light as air.
Stay true of heart and swift of mind,
Or be forever, lost and blind.

Lost in the Depths of Silence

In quiet depths where shadows dwell,
The silence weaves a secret spell.
Bubbles rise to greet the night,
As echoes fade from fading light.

A treasure chest of memories lost,
In silent depths, we pay the cost.
Each whisper soft, like drifting sand,
A world untouched by human hand.

The stillness wraps like velvet threads,
Ensnaring thoughts that dance in heads.
As creatures glide with graceful ease,
They carry tales upon the breeze.

Should one descend into the black,
Be wary, dear, there's no way back.
For silence holds a haunting song,
And calls you deep where you belong.

Luminous Echoes of the Abyss

In darkness where the colors bloom,
The creatures weave their paths of gloom.
With candlelight from tiny fins,
The ocean sings where silence spins.

Each flicker tells a story bright,
Of sunken ships and lost starlight.
Resounding through the depths they ring,
The songs of all who dared to sing.

Through murky depths, the echoes flow,
A symphony of ebb and woe.
In tangled weeds, the legends grow,
A luminous world we hardly know.

So venture forth where shadows loom,
And chase the light through ocean's gloom.
For every whisper in the dark,
Is but a trace of something stark.

Murmuring Depths of the Sea's Soul

Beneath the waves, a world of lore,
Where dreams and tides collide once more.
The sea's soul hums a soothing tune,
Beneath the watchful gaze of moon.

In shifting sands and fleeting rays,
It tells of love and lost romances.
Of ships once proud that sailed the brine,
Left only whispers, almost divine.

A murmuring call, a gentle plea,
From depths unknown, a mystic sea.
With each loud crash and soft retreat,
The ocean's heart begins to beat.

So wander near, and listen close,
To secrets that the waters boast.
For in the depths, beneath the swell,
There lies a magic none can quell.

Glistening Shadows Beneath the Waves

In depths of azure, shadows play,
Glimmers glisten, bright as day.
Mysteries dance in watery light,
Whispers lost, beyond our sight.

Coral castles, grand and old,
Guard secrets that they once foretold.
Fins flicker, weaving through dreams,
As the ocean softly gleams.

Bubbles rise; tales escape,
Of sunken ships and tangled fate.
Mermaids laugh in shimmering foam,
Where salty breezes call them home.

In moonlit depths, old songs will coil,
Of treasure lost and forgotten toil.
Where shadows linger, spirits roam,
In the cradle of the sea, their home.

So dive into the depths so wide,
With glistening shadows as your guide.
For the ocean whispers, old and wise,
In the shimmering dance beneath the skies.

Echoes of Midnight in the Deep Blue

At midnight's edge, the tide does swell,
Carrying secrets, we cannot tell.
Echoes murmur with waves' soft breath,
Of dreams entwined in ancient death.

The night is thick with stories spun,
Of battles lost and victories won.
Beneath the moon's silver embrace,
The ocean cradles time and space.

Stars above wink in soft delight,
As shadows frolic in velvet night.
A ship's lone cry breaks the calm,
A siren's song, a haunting balm.

In these waters, shadows blend,
With tales of lovers, lost and penned.
Each echo carries a flickering flame,
Of whispered hopes and forgotten names.

So linger here in twilight's glow,
Where echoes dance and secrets flow.
In the heart of night, the sea does sing,
Of endless wonders, hope, and spring.

Lost Whispers of the Ocean's Heart

In the depths, where silence sleeps,
The ocean's heart, a place that keeps.
Lost whispers drift on currents strong,
In depths where night and water belong.

Each wave a tale of time's embrace,
Of ancient mariners, lost in space.
Their voices linger in salty air,
Clinging softly to realms rare.

Seashells cradle stories deep,
Secrets of promises they keep.
Buried treasures, both dark and bright,
Await the curious hearts of night.

Fathoms thick with muted pain,
Where tiny flukes and tales remain.
A world unseen by those ashore,
With whispers gentle, forevermore.

So close your eyes, and dive within,
To find the salvaged hopes and sin.
For in this realm, your heart will start,
To hear the lost whispers of the heart.

Sirens' Secrets in Starlit Tides

Beneath the stars, the sirens play,
In starlit tides that sweep away.
Their laughter echoes, sweet as dew,
Guiding sailors to secrets new.

With shimmering scales and eyes like fire,
They sing old songs of lost desire.
A haunting melody fills the air,
Pulling hearts in, unaware.

In twilight's arms, their wiles take hold,
Of dreams and journeys yet untold.
Eyes aglow with ocean's gleam,
Dancing, weaving through each dream.

The tidal pull, a mystery,
Carries whispers across the sea.
With every wave, a tale is spun,
Of lovers lost and battles won.

So heed the call of the starlit tide,
Where sirens sing, and wishes bide.
For in their depths, the secrets lie,
In the dance of waves and the moonlit sky.

Waves of Memory in the Midnight Hour

In the quiet of night, whispers arise,
Echoes of laughter, beneath starry skies.
Moments like treasures, adrift on the sea,
Tides of remembrance, flowing to me.

Forgotten adventures, now softly revered,
In the waves of the past, both cherished and feared.
Fragments of joy, like shimmering pearls,
Drifting through dreams, where the heart unfurls.

Shadows may linger, but light breaks the dawn,
Revealing the paths that we've wandered upon.
Each ripple a story, each crash a refrain,
In the midnight hour, where memories reign.

So I stand on the shore, with the moon as my guide,
Capturing moments where memories abide.
Waves of emotion, both tender and bright,
Weaving the fabric of this magical night.

Dark Waters and Fleeting Dreams

Beneath the moon's gaze, where darkness does creep,
Lie secrets and sorrows, in shadows they seep.
The waters are restless, turbulent, deep,
Cradling whispers of what we can't keep.

Fleeting dreams dance like phantoms in flight,
Fading in silence, surrendering to night.
With each surge of tide, they echo and wail,
Lost in the depths, they drift like a sail.

Yet hope lingers gently, a flickering flame,
Guiding the lost to reclaim their own name.
For even in darkness, the stars shine above,
A promise of dawn, a testament of love.

So fear not the waters, though eerie they seem,
For through every shadow, a glimmer will beam.
Embrace the unknown, let your spirit roam,
In dark waters deep, you may find your way home.

Sirens in the Shadows of the Tide

Hark to the call of the sirens' sweet song,
Luring the hearts that have wandered too long.
In shadows they dance with a shimmer of grace,
Evoking desires, time can't erase.

Beneath the pale moonlight, their voices entwined,
Blend tales of enchantment with paths unaligned.
With each gentle swell, they beckon and plea,
Promising wonders that no one can see.

Yet heed well their warning, for some song may mislead,
Enticing the dreamers who follow their lead.
In the depths of the tide, where the brave might lose sight,

The sirens await, in the stillness of night.

But know, in the darkness, a choice must be made,
To linger or wander in shadows that fade.
For every sweet promise, a price may be paid,
In the depths of the sea, where legends are laid.

The Abyss that Binds

In the depths of the ocean, where silence prevails,
Lies an abyss that whispers forgotten tales.
With currents so strong, they pull and they twine,
Binding the stories that fate intertwines.

A catacomb of memories, both sorrow and light,
Drifting like shadows, obscured from our sight.
Yet in the darkness, a flicker is found,
A thread of connection that pulls us around.

For we are all woven from strands of the past,
Each moment a wave, too precious to cast.
In the depths of our hearts, we search and we yearn,
For the echoes of love, to which we return.

Though the abyss may be daunting, we venture with care,

Seeking the treasures that lie deep in there.
For in embracing the shadows, we learn to be free,
Bound by the wisdom of all that we see.

Siren's Lullaby beneath the Abyss

In depths where whispers softly hum,
The sirens sing their beckoning drum.
Their voices swirl like misty tides,
A haunting beauty where the darkness hides.

With silver scales that shimmer bright,
They lure the hearts in endless night.
Their lullabies weave through the deep,
Promising dreams that none shall keep.

Moonlit echoes ripple and dance,
Each note a spell, a fateful chance.
The currents pull with gentle kiss,
But drown in depths where hopes dismiss.

Beneath the waves, secrets lie still,
Of vanished souls and unheard shrill.
The sirens call, a siren's plea,
To join their song beneath the sea.

Yet in their song, a truth unfolds,
Of love and loss, of tales retold.
In silence, hearts must learn to cope,
For sirens sing of shattered hope.

Enigmatic Shadows in a Darkened Pool

Beneath the ripples, shadows play,
Enigmas whisper, night and day.
In pools of ink where secrets thrive,
A world of darkness comes alive.

Figures twist in patterns strange,
Drawing thoughts that slowly change.
Reflections murmur, old and wise,
In the depths, truth wears a guise.

Time stands still, caught in this phase,
Ghostly echoes of ancient days.
With every ripple, silence claims,
The heart that beats in whispered names.

A veil of mist, a fleeting glance,
Each shadow beckons with its dance.
Through murky depths, we seek to find,
The mysteries left behind.

So peer within this fateful pool,
Embrace the unknown, embrace the duel.
For shadows hold the stories grand,
Of those who dared to understand.

Secrets of the Cursed Lagoon

In twilight's grip, the waters dark,
A cursed lagoon, a hidden arc.
Where whispered tales of sailors lost,
Echo the waves, at a great cost.

The trees that lean with weary sighs,
Stand as witnesses to countless cries.
Their roots entwined with silent bones,
Guard secrets kept, yet never known.

Flickering lights like fireflies dance,
Luring hearts with a dreamy trance.
Yet shadows grow where laughter fades,
In silken mist, the truth invades.

With every breath, a tale unfolds,
Of treasures sought and dreams sold.
But in this land of murky fate,
Lies wisdom born from grief and hate.

So tread with care, O wanderer bold,
For treasures lie where stories are told.
In cursed waters, both sweet and vile,
Secrets await, cloaked in a smile.

Twilight Dances in the Ocean's Embrace

As twilight falls and shadows blend,
The ocean's arms begin to bend.
To cradle dreams upon the shore,
Where hopes resound forevermore.

The waves caress the golden sand,
With whispers soft, they make their stand.
Each crest a promise, each lull a song,
In ocean's embrace where we belong.

Stars awaken in the dusky hue,
Casting spells of glimmering blue.
As twilight dances, magic sows,
The heart of ocean gently glows.

Beneath the surface, wonders sleep,
In coral gardens, deep secrets keep.
In harmony, the night unfolds,
The ocean's tales through silence told.

So let us waltz with the setting sun,
In twilight's warmth, our souls as one.
For in this dance of ebb and flow,
The ocean's love forever grows.

The Dance of Ebon Threads and Moonlight

In twilight's hush, the shadows play,
Ebon threads in moonlight sway.
Whispers soft like secrets shared,
In this magic, hearts are bared.

Glimmers weave through branches bare,
Dancing lightly in the air.
Stars above begin to tease,
Softly murmuring with the breeze.

Crickets chirp a crimson tune,
As night enfolds the silver moon.
In the dark, the wild spirits meet,
With twinkling laughter, pure and sweet.

Close your eyes and feel the song,
Where the ancients once belonged.
Ebon threads in patterns flow,
In this dance, let your spirit glow.

So twirl beneath the watchful gaze,
Of luminous orbs in cosmic haze.
In the dance where dreams align,
Feel the pulse of magic divine.

Beneath the Veil of Celestial Currents

Beneath the veil of velvet skies,
Where stardust weaves a soft surprise.
Celestial currents twist and glide,
Inviting hearts to soar and ride.

A cosmic tale of whispers spun,
Echoes of life, both lost and won.
Each twinkle tells of hopes anew,
In realms where wishes dare to brew.

Waves of light in endless flight,
Drawing dreams from day to night.
With every breath, a longing stirs,
As destiny and fate converge.

In the stillness, stories hum,
Secrets ancient, yet to come.
Underneath the astral dome,
Every spark feels like a home.

Through the tapestry of time,
Hear the universe slip and climb.
In gentle caress of cosmic glow,
Find the paths you're meant to know.

Tidal Riddles and Phantom Echoes

Tidal riddles crash and break,
As echoes rise from deep awake.
The ocean's song, both fierce and sweet,
Calls to wanderers with bare feet.

Beneath the waves, a world concealed,
Mysteries vast, to none revealed.
In depths where sunlight cannot reach,
Phantoms dance, their wisdom teach.

Whirlpools twist with restless grace,
In silver foam, the shadows race.
With every swell, a secret stirs,
Whispered soft as ocean blurs.

The moonlit tide, a guiding hand,
Washing dreams upon the sand.
In rippling echoes, truths entwined,
Lead us gently, hearts aligned.

Oceans hold the tales of lore,
From shore to shore, they ever soar.
In tidal rhythm, life unfolds,
A dance of wonders, brave and bold.

Shadows of the Deep, Calling Forth

Shadows linger, deep and wide,
In the echoes where dreams abide.
Whispers soft, in twilight's breath,
Calling forth what lies in depth.

Ghostly figures weave and wend,
Through the murk, they twist and bend.
Illusions wrap like velvet night,
Holding secrets out of sight.

Flickering lights, a guide to roam,
In the dark, we find our home.
Through shifting veils, intentions speak,
To the brave who dare to seek.

With open hearts, the shadows sing,
In their dance, the lost take wing.
Every pause and every line,
Tells of fate in threads divine.

Shadows beckon with a call,
In their arms, we rise, we fall.
To face the unknown, pure and true,
In the depths, find the essence of you.

The Lure of the Abyssal Night

In shadows deep, where whispers dwell,
The moonlight weaves a haunting spell.
With every wave, a longing sigh,
The ocean calls, the heart will try.

Beneath the veil of starlit dreams,
The darkened sea is not as it seems.
A siren's song, both sweet and grim,
Beckons sailors, urging them in.

Their hearts, like lanterns, flicker bright,
Yet lose themselves in endless night.
A dance of shadows, twirl and spin,
The lure of darkness draws them in.

But in the depths, a price is paid,
For souls entwined in love's charade.
With every note, the tide will rise,
To swallow dreams and drown the cries.

So heed the whispers of the sea,
For there, the truth, your heart may flee.
In abyssal night, beware the bliss,
For lost to darkness, you'll find your kiss.

Lost Sirens of the Starlit Depths

In oceans blue, where dreams are spun,
The sirens wail, their song's begun.
With golden hair and eyes like fire,
They weave a tale that pulls you higher.

But in their eyes, a sorrow lies,
For starlit depths conceal goodbyes.
Each note a tear, each chord a plea,
For love once lost beneath the sea.

The sailor's heart, so brave yet frail,
Is drawn into their haunting tale.
With whispered words and tender grace,
They lead him to a shadowed place.

Yet as he slips beneath the wave,
He finds that he cannot be saved.
For every song holds shades of grief,
And depths of loss in their belief.

So turn away from siren's lure,
For love in darkness must endure.
In starlit depths, their echoes fade,
But hearts entwined in sorrow stayed.

Veins of Ebon in Ocean's Heart

In waters dark, where secrets lie,
The veins of ebon pulse and sigh.
A heart beats strong beneath the waves,
Each throb a tale, each beat a grave.

The ebb and flow of tides long lost,
Reflect the dreams that fate has tossed.
In depths unknown, the shadows creep,
Where sailors tread, in silence sweep.

A world concealed in midnight's grasp,
Where every whisper needs its clasp.
With tendrils deep, the ocean sways,
To guide the lost through twilight's maze.

Yet in the dark, a flicker burns,
A hope that through the night returns.
With courage forged in fear's embrace,
To seek the light in that dark place.

So when the heart feels lost at sea,
Remember, it can still be free.
Within the depths, a truth will rise,
To light the dark with azure skies.

The Siren's Secret Sanctuary

Beyond the mist, where waters gleam,
A sanctuary holds the dream.
In tranquil pools and coral beds,
The sirens hide their ancient threads.

With shells that shimmer, tales retold,
In safety's arms, their hearts unfold.
But whispers linger in the air,
Of joy entwined with hidden despair.

Upon the shores, the sailors wait,
To find the lure of love and fate.
But in the sanctuary's embrace,
A tempest brews, a fateful trace.

In laughter sweet, a sorrow wakes,
As tides of love reveal their stakes.
For every song that fills the night,
Can lead to paths of loss and fright.

So tread with care on sacred ground,
Where sirens sing and dreams are found.
In hidden depths, where shadows play,
The siren's heart may lead you astray.

Hidden Lullabies of the Brine

Beneath the waves, whispers gleam,
Echoes of dreams in the ocean's seam.
Softly they sigh, like a gentle breeze,
Carried by currents, with effortless ease.

Moonlit shadows dance on the sand,
Secrets are cradled in the sea's hand.
A lullaby sung by the coral blue,
Melodies woven with each tide's cue.

In twilight depths where the light does fade,
Mysteries linger, in silence laid.
Crimson fish glide where the ancients dwell,
In aquatic realms, their stories swell.

A sailor's heart may long for land,
But in the brine, a magic so grand.
Hidden lullabies, soft and bright,
Guide weary souls through the endless night.

So listen close to the ocean's breath,
Her lullabies wrapped in the cloak of death.
For in the tide, where the dark things weave,
Lie gentle songs that the waves believe.

Murmurs of the Deep's Lull

Down in the depths, the whispers swell,
Murmurs of stories that oceans tell.
With each swell, the water sighs,
As moonbeams dance in the darkened skies.

The seaweed sways with a soothing grace,
Embracing secrets in their embrace.
Gentle tides rock to a rhythmic scheme,
Where shadows and light play in a dream.

In the quietness, the echoes beckon,
A timeless charm that weaves a reckoning.
Pets of the deep in shimmering thrall,
Hear the beckoning of their call.

Bubbles burst like laughter, light and free,
Floating softly, a rare jubilee.
Murmurs wrap round like silk so tight,
Cradling wanderers through the night.

Curious hearts may sail afar,
But the deep's lull sings, a guiding star.
In the shadows where the water glows,
Find the peace only the ocean knows.

Secrets of the Celestial Arch

Above the waves, where the starlight weeps,
Lies a vault of secrets the ocean keeps.
Celestial whispers on a silken tide,
Mysteries hidden where shadows glide.

A canopy woven with silver thread,
Stories of stardust and dreams long dead.
Orbs of light dance on watery glass,
Reflecting glimpses of ages past.

The sky bends low, to kiss the sea,
Embracing silence with tender glee.
Crickets hum to the moon's soft glow,
While secrets of the arch ebb and flow.

In twilight's hush, where dreams alight,
Find your solace in the deep of night.
For every wave harbors a tale,
Spun in the stars, where wonders sail.

So listen well, let your soul take flight,
In the celestial dance of the ocean's light.
Guarded by time, yet timelessly fair,
Are secrets of night in the watery lair.

Crystalline Enigma of the Deep Sea

In the deep sea's heart lies a crystalline gleam,
An enigma wrapped in the ocean's dream.
Shimmering shards and echoes profound,
Where ancient wisdom in silence is found.

Jewel-toned fish dart through the blue,
Each movement echoes a truth yet new.
In the shadows, their dance is a song,
Weaving the tales of where they belong.

The currents whisper forgotten lore,
Of celestial beings and timbers that roar.
With gentle grace, the deep sea unveils,
A story as old as the earth's own trails.

Unearthed by the light of the moonlit tide,
The enigma beckons, inviting the wide.
For in the heart of the ocean's embrace,
Lies a crystalline truth—filled with grace.

So plunge into depths, let the waves surround,
For the crystalline treasures in silence abound.
In the echoing dark, where mysteries reign,
Dive deep, dear heart, and embrace the arcane.

Mysteries Wrapped in Seafoam

Beneath the waves where secrets lie,
A siren's song drifts soft and shy.
The tides do whisper tales of yore,
Wrapped in seafoam, they seek the shore.

The stones remember currents' fate,
With every surge, they oscillate.
In shadows deep, the echoes weave,
A tapestry that few believe.

Old sailors speak of storms so grand,
Where time forgot to take a stand.
And in the depths, lost dreams still float,
A phantom's dance, a haunting note.

Anemones like thoughts entwined,
Reveal the truth that we can't find.
The ocean's heart, a silent guide,
Where mysteries in seafoam bide.

As twilight falls, the stars take flight,
Their glimmers spark the restless night.
A solace found in depths so rare,
Embracing longing with tender care.

Glimmers of Twilight in the Depths

In the cradle of the dusky seas,
Lies a world that wavers with the breeze.
Glimmers dance in the fading light,
Casting shadows, drawing night.

The sand reflects the stars above,
An echo of the world we love.
With each wave, the stories grow,
Of ancient ships and lovers' woe.

The bioluminescent secrets bloom,
Illuminating the ocean's gloom.
With tender grace, they swirl and twine,
In twilight's embrace, they intertwine.

Faint whispers trail where the shadows creep,
As time slows down in the ocean's deep.
In that stillness, hearts can share,
Secrets born of salty air.

Embers fade into the deep, dark sea,
Yet hope remains, wild and free.
For every dusk must yield to dawn,
In depths where ancient dreams are drawn.

Echoing Dreams beneath the Waves

Underneath a sapphire dome,
Echoing dreams find their home.
The lull of tide, a tender song,
Where memories fade, but hopes grow strong.

A fleeting glance of sunlit beams,
Awakens the heart where thought redeems.
Myriad voices gently blend,
As whispers of the sea descend.

In coral caverns, shadows play,
Revealing truths that drift away.
A tale once told in tranquil hues,
Reborn in echoes of ocean blues.

With every roll of lapping waves,
Ancient spirits stir, the sea braves.
In whispers soft, they share their dreams,
Beneath the depths, all truly seems.

So listen close as currents flow,
For in each ebb, and undertow,
Lie stories glimpsed in brine and foam,
Echoing dreams that call us home.

Shades of Midnight in Aquatic Whispers

In shades of midnight, shadows loom,
Aquatic whispers break the gloom.
Where twilight softens into night,
The ocean breathes, a hush of light.

Secrets swirl in the moon's embrace,
Each wave a line in nature's grace.
The stars above, like gems they gleam,
Reflecting all that lies unseen.

Luminous creatures glide with ease,
Dancing gently, on the breeze.
A shift in currents shapes the tales,
Of sailors lost in tempest gales.

In crystal caverns, time stands still,
Where silenced echoes chase their will.
The ocean's heart beats deep and strong,
In whispered lullabies, life belongs.

As night unfolds its velvet reign,
The sea reminds us of our pain.
Yet in its depths, the truth will find,
Shades of midnight call the kind.

Eclipsed Jewels of the Moonlit Sea

In the hush of night, they gleam,
Jewels cast from dreams,
Whispers of tides in the cool breeze,
Beneath the moon's gentle tease.

Waves that kiss the sandy shore,
Echo tales of ancient lore,
Merfolk dance, their laughter sweet,
In waters where the shadows meet.

Stars above, a twinkling guide,
To secrets where the sea-nymphs hide,
Reflecting silver on the swell,
In this enchanted, watery spell.

Pearls of wisdom tucked away,
Await the dawn's soft, golden ray,
With every ripple, dreams unfold,
Eclipsed jewels, treasures of old.

As the tide pulls, the heart sings,
Of whispered hopes and fragile things,
In moonlit reverie, we lay,
Beneath the waves, our hearts at play.

Luminous Trails of the Siren's Call

Beneath the waves, a song so clear,
Lures the hearts of all who hear,
Siren's voice, a melody bright,
Guides the lost through the starry night.

Rippling echoes on the sea,
Casting spells of ecstasy,
With every note, the waters dance,
Ensnaring souls in a trance.

Guiding ships through perilous tide,
Where shadows and mysteries abide,
Xanadu waits past rocky shores,
In the depths, adventure soars.

Luminous trails they weave with grace,
Drawing wanderers to embrace,
Secrets kept in depths profound,
In the siren's call, dreams are found.

But beware the price of the song,
For in its beauty, you may long,
To leave the land behind, oppressed,
By the lure of the ocean's chest.

Enchanted Reefs and Hidden Secrets

In the shallows, colors spin,
Coral castles where dreams begin,
Whispers float on shimmering tides,
Where ancient magic softly hides.

Creatures dance in vibrant hues,
A realm where the sea's heart pursues,
Air filled with charms of the deep,
A world where lost promises sleep.

Beneath the waves, in shadowed nooks,
Lie treasures lost in storybooks,
Adventures waiting to be told,
In the reefs where the brave are bold.

Mysterious paths lead deep within,
Where light and darkness twine and spin,
Nature's wonders, a splendid sight,
In the depths, the hidden brighten.

Echoes of laughter in salty spray,
Invite the dreamers who stray,
To seek what lies in the ocean's keep,
In enchanted reefs, secrets seep.

Veils of Darkness in Aquatic Realms

In the depths where shadows creep,
Veils of darkness, secrets keep,
Ghostly shapes of past regrets,
In the aquatic realm, no one forgets.

Eerie silence wraps the sea,
Where unseen eyes gaze longingly,
The currents hum a ghostly song,
In this world, where phantoms throng.

Lost souls swim through ancient fears,
Their whispered cries, a melody of tears,
A labyrinth of dreams denied,
In the depths where shadows abide.

Glimmers of light break through the veil,
As the haunted whisper their tale,
Of battles fought in aquatic gloom,
And the longing for eternal bloom.

Yet in the dark, a spark remains,
Hope flickers amidst the chains,
In these realms where silence reigns,
Veils of darkness, yet love gains.

Tides of Midnight and Lost Souls

In shadows deep where secrets dwell,
The whispers float like distant bells.
Beneath the moon's soft glowing light,
The tides of midnight grip the night.

Lost souls wander with haunting grace,
In search of peace, a warm embrace.
Their stories told in gentle sighs,
As starlit hopes begin to rise.

The ocean's breath, a lullaby,
Carries dreams that dare to fly.
With every wave, a tale unfolds,
Of love and loss, of hearts so bold.

Yet as the dawn begins to break,
The spell of night begins to shake.
Those tides will wane, the shadows fade,
While memories in sunlight wade.

But in the hush of twilight's seam,
We find the courage to redeem.
For every tide must rise and fall,
A dance of fate that binds us all.

Reflections of Crystal Waters

In crystal waters, secrets hide,
Mirroring dreams where hope resides.
Each ripple whispers tales of old,
Of lost desires and hearts of gold.

The sky reflects in liquid blue,
With clouds that linger like a view.
Beneath the surface, memories dwell,
In watery depths, they weave their spell.

The gentle breeze caresses light,
As shadows twist in soft delight.
And suddenly, the world grows still,
As time bows down to nature's will.

Yet even still, the waters change,
With tides that ebb and rearrange.
Each glance reveals a hidden truth,
A dance of wisdom, age, and youth.

So let us gaze with hearts laid bare,
At crystal waters, pure and rare.
For in their depths, a world awaits,
Of dreams and wishes, love, and fates.

The Call of the Hidden Abyss

In the heart of night, a call does rise,
From abysses deep, beneath dark skies.
With every pulse, the currents sway,
Enigmas dance where shadows play.

The ocean's breath, a haunting song,
Drawn to places where souls belong.
In secrets drenched, the waters cry,
With longing deep as the starry sky.

A compass lost, but spirits find,
The hidden paths that fate has lined.
Through caves of whispers, dreams are spun,
Where light and dark unite as one.

Yet courage blooms in depths so wide,
Embracing fears that long have tried.
For even there, 'neath waves of doubt,
The heart of hope will find its route.

So heed the call, and dive within,
To discover where true journeys begin.
For in the abyss, we will see,
The strength of souls that dare to be.

Soft Murmurs of the Deep

In quiet depths where silence breathes,
Soft murmurs rise like gentle leaves.
The secrets of the sea unfold,
In notes of azure, tales of gold.

With every wave, a lullaby,
Of dreams that drift and softly sigh.
The ocean's heart, a soothing balm,
Embracing all in its quiet calm.

From sunlit shores to kelp-strewn beds,
Where life abounds and journey spreads.
In swirling currents, stories spin,
Of every fight, of every win.

Yet in the night, when stars take flight,
The whispers deepen, soft and bright.
They weave a spell, a mantle fine,
Connecting hearts, the yours and mine.

So come, dear friend, and take a peek,
At soft murmurs that gently speak.
For in their depths, the beauty lies,
Where all our hopes eternally rise.

Midnight Fantasies and Ebon Gloom

In shadows deep where dreams might soar,
The whispers call from ancient lore.
A moonlit path unfolds its might,
A dance of spirits, pure delight.

With every breath a magic spun,
As time melts down, we become one.
The stars above weave tales so grand,
Of realms unseen, both wild and planned.

In darkness blooms a silver flower,
Empowered by the midnight hour.
The echoes speak of hopes untold,
In ebon gloom, our hearts behold.

Treasures waiting, left to find,
Within the shadows, intertwined.
A flicker here, a shimmer bright,
Awakens dreams in endless night.

So leap with joy, embrace the night,
For magic stirs in every flight.
In fantasies where wishes gleam,
We find our truth, we craft our dream.

The Heart of the Ocean's Abyss

Beneath the waves, a world unfolds,
Where stories sleep, and time grows cold.
In depths where sunlight fears to tread,
The heart of dreams is softly spread.

A siren's song, both sweet and rare,
Draws wanderers to ocean's lair.
In whispers wrapped, the currents sigh,
In tangled hopes, our spirits fly.

The shipwrecked tales of love and loss,
Are buried deep beneath the gloss.
With every tide that ebbs and flows,
The secrets of the deep ocean rose.

Among the coral, colors bright,
Reside the memories of the night.
In every ripple, shadows blend,
A dance of souls that never end.

So dive within the briny sea,
To find the truth that sets us free.
For in the depths, our hearts reside,
In ocean's pulse, our dreams abide.

Beneath the Unseen Currents

Beneath the waves where silence reigns,
The unseen currents weave their chains.
In hidden depths, the secrets lie,
A soft embrace, a gentle sigh.

Tides undulate, a whispered tune,
Beneath the glow of the silver moon.
In shadows deep, our hopes entwine,
As fate's design begins to shine.

Each drop of water holds a dream,
A fleeting thought, a riddle's theme.
The ebbing night, a silent guide,
In unseen paths where souls abide.

Through tangled weeds and drifting sands,
Awaits a world that understands.
The rhythm pulls our hearts anew,
In currents dark, we find our hue.

So heed the call of depths unknown,
In ocean's grasp, we find our own.
For every wave that breaks the shore,
Whispers of magic and so much more.

Shards of Memory Hidden Deep

In corners dark where shadows creep,
Lie shards of memory, buried deep.
Each fragment glimmers, lost yet clear,
A tapestry of joy and fear.

The past's embrace, a double-edged sword,
In quiet moments, truths restored.
With every breath, we sift through time,
In every note, a silent rhyme.

The ghosts of laughter linger still,
As heartbeats echo with a thrill.
In memories' vault, the heart will seek,
The gentle touch of voices weak.

But through the ache, there's beauty found,
A symphony of love unbound.
In shadows cast, we dance and play,
Reclaim the light, we find our way.

So gather all your dreams so dear,
For in the dark, they'll reappear.
With every shard, a story gleams,
In hidden depths of faded dreams.

Whispers from the Depths of the Tide

Beneath the waves, a secret sigh,
Where shadows dance and silence lie,
A melody from ages past,
In ocean's heart, the spells are cast.

The moonlight kisses every crest,
As sirens weave their silent jest,
They call to souls who once were free,
In depths of blue, their legacy.

The currents churn with ancient lore,
They speak of ships that sailed before,
Each whisper tells of fate entwined,
With ocean's depths, their dreams aligned.

In twilight's glow, the waters gleam,
Such is the power of their dream,
Beneath the tide, where spirits play,
A world concealed, yet bright as day.

So heed the songs that ebb and flow,
For in those whispers, truth may glow,
The depths hold tales both dark and bright,
Be drawn, dear heart, into the night.

Echoes of Lost Navigation

The compass spins, a muted sound,
In endless seas, our fates are bound,
With charts that crumble, lost from sight,
We sail through shadows, grasping light.

Each star above, a ghostly guide,
In tempest's heart, we must abide,
The voyages of hearts untrue,
Can lead to shores of skies so blue.

Through tangled maps of time and tide,
We search for truth, with hearts as wide,
Yet whispers of the past remain,
Like echoes of a soft refrain.

With sails of hope, we chase the dawn,
In dreams of journeys yet to spawn,
The winds of fate will push and pull,
Through silent nights, the soul is full.

Each journey's path must find its way,
Through darkened storms and light of day,
For lost navigation finds its course,
In hearts that seek with boundless force.

Chasms of Dreaming Night

In velvet dark, where shadows creep,
The dreams are spun, the secrets keep,
Beneath the veil of timeless schemes,
Awake, we dance in silent dreams.

Each flicker holds a cosmic chance,
In every star, a mystic dance,
The chasms deep where wishes lie,
In midnight's hold, our spirits fly.

The rhythm of the night will call,
Through whispers soft, we'll rise and fall,
The cloak of starlight drapes us near,
As echoes ring, the heart will steer.

In boundless realms, the mind will roam,
Through hidden paths, we find our home,
In chasms wide, where secrets play,
The dreamers weave the night away.

So take my hand, let visions soar,
In dreaming night, we'll seek the shore,
Where time dissolves and shadows meld,
In depths of night, our fates are held.

The Lament of the Drowned

Amidst the waves, the lost ones weep,
For dreams unchained, in silence deep,
With weary hearts, they haunt the foams,
The sea's embrace, their final homes.

In moonlit hours, their voices rise,
A haunting song beneath the skies,
Each tear they shed a tale of woe,
Of love and loss, a heart's deep throe.

The currents carry tales of plight,
Of ships that vanished in the night,
Yet in the depths, a truth remains,
A love unbroken, bound by chains.

So listen close when storm winds howl,
In whispered breath, their spirits prowl,
For every wave that breaks ashore,
Holds stories lost, forevermore.

With every tide, the mourners sigh,
Their echoes drift in ghostly cry,
The ocean holds their bitter crown,
In sorrow sweet, the drowned's lament.

The Siren's Lament in Ink-black Waters

Beneath the waves where shadows creep,
A siren sings, her secrets deep.
Her voice, a haunting, ethereal grace,
Echoes softly in that darkened space.

Ink-black waters, where dreams entwine,
Whispers of fate in the depths confine.
Her heart is fierce, yet tender still,
Bound by the current, she bends to its will.

Lost sailors drift, pulled by her song,
To the depths where they no longer belong.
Eyes of the abyss reflect their fears,
As the siren's call draws forth their tears.

In shimmering tides, their hopes collide,
A dance of despair in the ocean wide.
For every note that stirs the air,
Is a spell woven from longing and care.

Yet in her lament, a longing stays,
A wish for freedom that never decays.
For in her depths, the shadows swell,
As she sings of the tales that no one can tell.

Abyssal Reflections of a Hidden Realm

In the stillness of the moonlit sea,
Lie tales of the deep, whispering free.
Reflections shimmer on water's face,
Revealing a world, a hidden place.

Beneath the surface, secrets bloom,
Crafted in darkness, consumed by gloom.
Ghostly figures dance in the night,
Drifting softly without a fright.

Layers of shadows, entwined and bold,
Mark the passage of stories untold.
An endless journey through time and space,
Where dreams and reality find their grace.

Glimmers of hope in an endless void,
Where memories linger, never destroyed.
Each reflection a portal, each wave a sigh,
In that hidden realm where spirits fly.

And with every echo, a truth is spun,
Binding together what's lost, what's begun.
In the heart of the abyss, truths intertwine,
As reflections reveal what once was divine.

Treasures Wrapped in Shimmering Darkness

Amidst the tide's gentle embrace,
Lies treasure cloaked in shadowed grace.
Glistening gems in the blackened sea,
Whispers of magic, wild and free.

Each pearl a story, each shell a clue,
Of wondrous secrets that none ever knew.
Crafted by time and moonlight's caress,
In this realm of enchantment, nothing less.

Crystalline echoes of laughter sweet,
Dance on the waves, a rhythmic beat.
The ocean's bounty, both dark and bright,
Holds ancient lore in its shimmers of light.

Treasures await in the depths below,
In caverns where only the brave dare go.
For those who seek with hearts so bold,
Will find the magic the waters hold.

Yet beware the shadows that twist and sway,
As darkness beckons with soft dismay.
For every treasure, a price must be paid,
In the depths of the sea where secrets are laid.

Cursed Melodies of the Abyss

In the murmur of waves, a song so dire,
A cursed melody, laced with fire.
Haunting notes that chill the bone,
Echo through waters forever alone.

The abyss hums with tales of woe,
Of those who ventured to depths below.
Their laughter lost in the tide's cruel clutch,
While the sirens sing, they don't feel much.

Each haunting chord, a story weaves,
Of souls entrapped in endless leaves.
In darkness cradled, their spirits rise,
Pairing their sighs with the night's soft cries.

Cursed by the depths where the lost can't roam,
They sing the anthems of a watery home.
And though their voices shimmer and blend,
In the heart of the storm, they find no end.

So heed the call in the shadows' curl,
For darkened waves hide a mysterious whirl.
In cursed melodies, find solace or dread,
In the depths of the abyss, where dreams are fed.

The Siren's Enigma Beneath

Beneath the waves, a song so sweet,
Calls to sailors with hearts that meet.
In swirling depths, where secrets hide,
The truth resounds, like an ocean tide.

Her voice drifts softly on the breeze,
Luring souls to dance with ease.
In shimmering light, the shadows play,
By the siren's call, they lose their way.

Yet tales of woe in silence drown,
As moonbeams rise and gently frown.
For every dream that glimmers bright,
A peril waits in the dead of night.

What lies below in the argent waves?
A heart entangled, the soul it saves.
An enigma calls, the heart entwined,
In the darkened depths, the answers blind.

So heed the whispers that beckon near,
For laughter rings but hides the fear.
Choose wisely, dear ones, where you tread,
For love and loss lie close, instead.

Whispers in the Darkness of Deep Waters

In deepest dark, where silence reigns,
Whispers echo, entwined with chains.
The stillness pulses, a heartbeat's song,
A tale of wonder, where dreams belong.

Beneath the surface, secrets curl,
In the shadows, faint ripples swirl.
Softly spoke, the currents flow,
Bringing forth what we long to know.

Fish like shadows dance below,
Guarding stories wrapped in woe.
The night invites us to explore,
What lies beyond the ocean's door.

Beware the pull of haunted tides,
Where hidden treasures and danger hides.
For every whisper, a truth concealed,
In the depths, the heart is revealed.

So follow the call but tread with care,
For deep waters bear a weight of despair.
Yet in their depths, you may yet find,
The courage to challenge the ties that bind.

Shadows Within the Tidal Veil

In twilight's glow, where shadows creep,
The tidal veil holds secrets deep.
With every wave that breaks the shore,
A whispered tale, forevermore.

As moonlight dances on the sea,
Shimmers of truth, a mystery.
Faint echoes float on the ocean's breath,
A promise held in the clasp of death.

What lurks beneath the silhouette?
A haunting gaze we can't forget.
In swirling murk, the dreams reside,
With hopes and fears entwined inside.

The shadows beckon, soft and sly,
Through tides that fall and waves that fly.
In the depths, a story longs to weave,
Of love and loss few dare believe.

So dive into the dark to see,
The world beneath, the heart's decree.
For shadows dance in waters wide,
And life, dear friend, shall be your guide.

The Ocean's Veiled Heart

The ocean breathes, a gentle giant,
With mysteries wrapped in silence defiant.
In brimming depths, a heartbeat sways,
Holding a truth in its tender gaze.

Veiled in depths, her heart does beat,
A rhythm soft, yet tumultuous, sweet.
Each wave a sigh, each tide a tale,
Of sailors lost and love that pales.

Beneath the foam, where nightmares blend,
And whispered secrets won't transcend.
The currents shift, the waters change,
In shadows deep, we rearrange.

Yet hope arrives on the crest of dawn,
Where sunlight spills and fears are gone.
The heart of the ocean, vast and grand,
Holds mysteries eternal, like grains of sand.

So listen close and take the dare,
To seek the truth behind the glare.
For every wave that kisses shore,
Speaks of a heart that longs for more.

Starlit Secrets Underwater

In depths where the starlit whispers play,
The fish weave stories from the light of day.
Echoes of laughter, soft as a dream,
Swirl around coral, a magical gleam.

Secrets unfurl in shimmering tides,
Crabs dance along where the mystery hides.
In shadows of kelp, old tales come alive,
A kingdom of wonders beneath waves that thrive.

Behold the treasures where the mermaids dwell,
Each bubble a secret, each ripple a spell.
The water cradles all that is rare,
Glimmers of magic drift through the air.

In twilight's embrace, the currents will sing,
Of glittering dreams and what night may bring.
With every soft sway, the ocean does weave,
A tapestry woven for those who believe.

Dark Fables from the Abyss

From shadows that murmur with ancient dread,
Whispers of creatures long thought dead.
They tell of the tempest, the wrath of the sea,
And legends of sailors who wished to be free.

In blackened waters where nightmares crawl,
Fables forgotten behind fate's cold wall.
Each flicker of light, a story awoken,
Of promises made and of hearts that are broken.

A leviathan stirs, disturbed from its rest,
With secrets so dark, it knows every quest.
Yet hope lingers softly in depths far below,
Where shadows retreat and the bravest may go.

With inked maps in hand, they drift through the night,
Chasing the tales of the lost and the light.
For every dark fable holds kernels of truth,
In the depths of the ocean, the wisdom of youth.

Luminescence Beneath the Lagoon

Beneath the calm waters, a glow starts to rise,
With flickers of starlight brightening the skies.
Neon sea creatures dance with delight,
In the heart of the lagoon, where day turns to night.

Bioluminescent trails weave through the waves,
Guiding lost souls to the shores that it saves.
The rhythm of life, a gentle ballet,
Where dreams are awakened and shadows betray.

A lantern of hope shines bright from below,
Illuminating paths that the wanderers know.
In the depths of the lagoon, a symphony plays,
As water and light create wondrous displays.

Each ripple and shimmer, a brush with the past,
A promise that beauty and magic can last.
In the embrace of the water, we find our own song,
In luminescence strong, where we all still belong.

In the Grasp of the Ocean's Shadows

In the murky embrace where the light fades away,
The ocean's shadows begin to sway.
With secrets entwined in the depths of its hold,
Old stories awaken, both timid and bold.

A grip like a whisper weaves through the deep,
Calling to dreamers who swim, wake, and sleep.
The haunting calls echo, both eerie and sweet,
In the grasp of the shadows, their fates seem to meet.

The pulse of the tide, a heartbeat of lore,
Draws forth the brave souls to explore and implore.
In silence, they wander through currents that course,
Finding lost echoes in the ocean's discourse.

Deep in the dark, where the mysteries lie,
Beneath swirling waters, where shadows can fly.
The ocean holds tight to the dreams of the night,
In the grasp of its shadows, we find our own light.

A Symphony of Depth and Dusk

Beneath the waves, where shadows creep,
A symphony plays, both soft and deep.
Whispers of dusk, they twirl and weave,
In twilight's embrace, we quietly believe.

The ocean's breath, a haunting tune,
Under the watch of a silvery moon.
Ripples of night serenade the shore,
Echoes of secrets, forevermore.

Stars twinkle down with a gentle sigh,
Painting the heavens, a velvet sky.
Each note a wish, a dream set free,
In harmony's dance, just you and me.

As tides recede, the absent sound,
Of crabs and shells, on dampened ground.
In every wave, a story unfolds,
Of lovers lost and treasures untold.

So linger here, where time grows still,
In symphonies lost, and the heart's own thrill.
With dusk as our stage, we shall ignite,
An encore of dawn, a new day's light.

Carvings of the Deep's Silenced Tales

In ocean's grip, where shadows bloom,
Carvings of time, in silence loom.
Whispers of legends, chiseled in stone,
Each tide erases, yet leaves its clone.

Fables of mariners, brave and lost,
Embedded in depths, at a terrible cost.
The salt of their tears, the weight of regret,
Echoes of echoes, we cannot forget.

Waves crash and roll, with secrets to tell,
Carried on currents, they cast a spell.
Sunken ships cradle their haunting past,
In tales of the ocean, forever cast.

Each driftwood fragment, a memory wakes,
Of storms that raged and the quiet lakes.
Inscribed in the shells, the echoes remain,
A history woven with loss and gain.

So tread with care, on this sacred sand,
For every step holds a story unplanned.
The deep's silent tales, a treasure to seek,
In the heart of the ocean, the voices speak.

Veils of Twilight Cradled by the Sea

As daylight slips, the twilight veils,
A gentle hush where magic prevails.
Beneath the waves, a soft embrace,
Twilight whispers, a serene place.

Shells gather secrets, glistening bright,
In the twilight's glow, under the light.
Each grain of sand, a soft caress,
Where dusk cradles the world's excess.

The horizon blurs, where sea meets sky,
In veils of purple, where dreams can fly.
A flicker of gold, the last sun's kiss,
In every tide, an ocean's bliss.

Night draws near with a silken hand,
Weaving shadows across the strand.
The gulls take flight, their calls entwined,
In twilight's cradle, solace we find.

So linger long at the water's rim,
In this tranquil space, let your heart swim.
For in these veils, where dreams softly sigh,
The soul finds peace as the day bids goodbye.

The Murmurs of the Drowned and Forgotten

In the stillness deep, where memories dwell,
The murmurs rise from a shattered shell.
Voices of those who lost their way,
In the depths of blue, they silently sway.

Echoes of laughter, now faded and frail,
Stories of journeys where hope set sail.
With every wave, a sigh escapes,
From the hearts of the drowned, their unseen shapes.

Caught in the currents, they long to be heard,
Their dreams like whispers, soft and blurred.
With every tide, they plead for the sun,
In the realm of the deep, where shadows run.

Beneath the surface, a world left behind,
Where time dances on, unconfined.
The memories linger, like pearls in the sand,
A testament to lives that slip from hand.

So listen closely to the ocean's dark song,
For the drowned and forgotten still belong.
In the depths, they weave tales of sorrow and grace,
In the whispers of water, they find their place.

Depths of Enchantment and Dark Dreams

In the shadowed depths where secrets lie,
Whispers of magic float softly by.
Creatures of wonder twirl and spin,
Weaving their tales amid the din.

Glimmers of hope in the murky deep,
Hidden treasures the ocean will keep.
Bubbles of laughter, a siren's call,
Enchanting all who are drawn to enthrall.

Through currents that pulse like a heart's own beat,
Adventures await where sea legends meet.
In a world where the ordinary fades,
Imagination blooms in vibrant cascades.

Yet darker shadows may cloud the light,
Revealing the fears that lurk out of sight.
Dreams woven tight in the fabric of night,
Echoes of battles and mystical flight.

But courage ignites in the depths of us all,
With friends by our side, we'll rise and not fall.
For every enchantment and dream intertwined,
A story is told, proving hearts are aligned.

Midnight Glimmers on the Sea Floor

When the moon spills silver on the tide,
Stars dance above where the mysteries hide.
A chorus of waves sings soft lullabies,
As secrets breathe deep beneath starlit skies.

In the cool, calm depths, the magic will soar,
Midnight glimmers beckon from the ocean's core.
With each gentle stroke of a shimmering fin,
Possibilities endless, let adventures begin.

Jewel-toned fish weave a tapestry bright,
Lighting the dark with their radiant flight.
Together they spin in a celestial waltz,
Filling the abyss with shimmering pulse.

Reflections of dreams ripple through the night,
As shadows and wonders eclipse the starlight.
Echoes of laughter in the depths start to gleam,
Inviting us deeper into the dream stream.

So dive into realms where your heart can explore,
And dance with the glimmers on the sea floor.
For the night brings tales that are waiting in front,
As secrets unfold, it's the ocean we hunt.

Beneath the Coral's Veiled Embrace

In gardens where corals bloom and sway,
Life pulses gently in a colorful display.
Anemones dance while the sea turtles glide,
Beneath the coral's veiled embrace we hide.

Each crevice a realm, a home for the small,
Where lantern-fish flicker and rainbow-hued thrall.
The ocean's heartbeat whispers soft and clear,
Inviting our souls to linger near.

Enchanted moments blend hues bright and bold,
Stories of wonders in silence told.
As currents embrace, they twine like a dream,
In every color, life's rhythm will beam.

Yet shadows may creep through the coral's bright sheen,
A reminder that beauty can hide in the unseen.
But still, hope remains in this ocean's expanse,
Bringing together each glimmering chance.

So dwell in the depths, where magic is sown,
Beneath coral's embrace, we are never alone.
For beneath the surface, life flows like a stream,
In the heart of the ocean, we find our dream.

Luminous Nightfall in Aquatic Realms

As dusk draws its curtain over the tide,
The ocean awakens, a wondrous guide.
With luminous pearls that splatter the dark,
Each wave holds a secret, each ripple a spark.

Creatures of twilight break free from their dreams,
Glowing like lanterns in moon's silver beams.
In harmony moving, a soft serenade,
Beneath currents swirling, where fantasies aid.

A symphony whispers from depths far away,
Calling the dreamers to join in the play.
Tales twine like kelp in a magical dance,
Inviting enchantment, a curious glance.

Yet danger may lurk in the shimmering glow,
Mysteries tangled in waters below.
But courage ignites in the heart of the night,
As we journey together, fueled by delight.

For in aquatic realms where the echoes resound,
Luminous nightfall wraps us around.
Together we dive into hearts intertwined,
Finding solace and magic that brightens the mind.